NEW LIGHT

Award Winners

2003
Veronica Bailey
Polly Braden
Edgar Martins
Danny Treacy
Naglaa Walker

2004
Emma Hamilton
Travis Hodges
Sarah Lynch
Richard Page
Léonie Purchas

2005
Daniel Gustav Cramer
Nina Mangalanayagam
Oliver Parker
Sarah Pickering
Luke Stephenson

2006
Zoe Hatziyannaki
Peter Oetzmann
Indre Serpytyte
Paul Winch-Furness

2007
Sophie Gerrard
Ed Kevill-Davies
Moira Lovell
Kevin Newark
Dana Popa

2008
Alice Myers
James Pogson
Kurt Tong
Nicky Walsh
Martina Lindqvist

NEW LIGHT

JERWOOD PHOTOGRAPHY AWARDS 2003-08

Foreword by Roanne Dods
Director, Jerwood Charitable Foundation

Essay by Martin Barnes
Senior Curator, Photographs, Victoria and Albert Museum, London

Afterword by Gloria Chalmers
Editor, Portfolio Magazine

Portfolio Magazine

Jerwood Photography Awards 2008 exhibition at Impressions Gallery, Bradford, 15 February 2009. (Photo: Heather Johnson)

Foreword

Roanne Dods

Over my years working for the Jerwood Charitable Foundation, I have gained a real understanding of the alchemy that it takes to get an award right. By 'right' I mean attracting the quality of work and artists that you want, the level of reward and how it benefits the artists, and the right kind of critical response.

What makes it work is the clarity of purpose and therefore the brief, the quality of the people managing the project, and the setting through which the award is presented to the world. I have been so proud that we have been able to work so closely with Gloria Chalmers, Editor of Portfolio Magazine, to get it just right, for us and I hope, by implication, the artists.

The Jerwood Charitable Foundation had been itching to be more involved in the world of photography and to find a robust way of supporting artist photographers – we had already created different programmes and awards within painting, drawing, sculpture, applied arts and more conceptual work. I responded to a request from Portfolio Magazine to renew my subscription in 2002 and while saying yes, please, I suggested a meeting with the Editor – the magazine was one of the most beautiful, interesting, and high quality ventures in photography that I could see. I didn't know at the time but was not remotely surprised to understand that it was an award-winning enterprise, with a massive international reach, run by the quite outstanding Gloria Chalmers.

It was at the tail-end of the last dip in the markets in 2002 and budgets were tight. Gloria embraced the concept of supporting emerging artists with a rigour, passion, judgement and dedication that gave the Awards the depth and quality that make them what they are. The brief is tight, but it captures exactly the right point between artists leaving college and that difficult point at which they may contemplate giving up. The award is generous but it isn't daunting. The final exhibition is exhibited in London and at galleries throughout the UK, and has invaluable exposure in Portfolio Magazine. The artists are cared for, promoted, and supported throughout the whole process by Gloria and Portfolio. Each year, the artists become their own community. Each year, we have the privilege of working with outstanding selectors to witness the interests of each new group of immensely talented photographers at a very particular point in time.

I am thrilled to see this particular group presented in this way, and I hope you enjoy their work and take your interest in it further. Thank you to each of the artists to agreeing to be involved in this book. Many have gone on to huge success and I am thrilled that we can present all the work in this way. I would like to thank Martin Barnes enormously for setting the context in this book. It is Gloria though that I would like to thank for making these awards the success that they are.

Roanne Dods is Director of the Jerwood Charitable Foundation.

Selectors

2003
Mark Haworth-Booth, Visiting Professor of Photography, University of the Arts London
Catherine Yass, Visual Artist
David Chandler, Director, Photoworks
Amanda Hopkinson, Writer and Critic
Gloria Chalmers, Editor, Portfolio Magazine

2004
John Gill, Independent Curator
Duncan Forbes, Senior Curator of Photography, National Galleries of Scotland
Alexa Wright, Visual Artist
Amna Malik, Writer
Gloria Chalmers, Editor, Portfolio Magazine

2005
Andrew Dewdney, Educationalist and Writer
Patrick Henry, Director, Open Eye Gallery, Liverpool
Val Williams, Writer and Curator
Bettina von Zwehl, Visual Artist
Gloria Chalmers, Editor, Portfolio Magazine

2006
Russell Roberts, Senior Research Fellow in Photography, University of Wales, Newport
David A Bailey, Senior Photography Curator, Autograph, London
Francis Hodgson, Head of Photography, Sotheby's, London
Sian Bonnell, Visual Artist
Gloria Chalmers, Editor, Portfolio Magazine

2007
Martin Barnes, Senior Curator, Photographs, Victoria and Albert Museum, London
Gayle Chong Kwan, Visual Artist
Anne McNeill, Director, Impressions Gallery, Bradford
John Davies, Artist/Photographer
Gloria Chalmers, Editor, Portfolio Magazine

2008
Dewi Lewis, Dewi Lewis Publishing
Neeta Madahar, Visual Artist
David Scull, Director, Hoopers Gallery, London
Marta Weiss, Curator, Photographs, Victoria and Albert Museum, London
Gloria Chalmers, Editor, Portfolio Magazine

Celebration and Reflection
Jerwood Photography Awards 2003-08

Martin Barnes

From the beginning of the 1990s, until the present, photography has taken centre stage in the world of contemporary art as never before. The instigation of the annual Jerwood Photography Awards in 2003 was therefore both prescient and timely. Each year, the Award has been promoted and made accessible through a prestigious prize-giving evening, an accompanying touring exhibition, and the publication of the winners' works, complimented by a critical essay, in Portfolio Magazine. These yearly outcomes marked and supported the energy and creativity of some of the best emerging talents in the field.

It is now time to celebrate and reflect on the cumulative effect of this Award. This book provides a fitting opportunity to do so, gathering all the Award winners together for the first time. It provides a fascinating look at the fresh, innovative and varied bodies of work to have emerged from visual art degree courses in the UK over the last six years. This publication is not only a milestone in the life of the Award; it can also be seen as a sampler – highlighting an exemplary cross-section of styles, approaches and personal voices – giving a valuable insight into a pivotal moment in the history of photography.

Selecting

The Award has centred primarily on the fine art of creative photography used for personal artistic expression, rather than photographs that are primarily intended as illustrations, advertising, editorial or commercial work, or as a demonstration of technical skill. Evocative projects of photojournalism have formed an impressive adjunct to this predominant fine art tendency. The choices reflect the focus of the Award, embodied by the collective interests of the balanced and changing panel of selectors, consisting of artists, curators, writers, publishers and educationalists.

In the selecting process each body of work is tested from many angles, from the technical to the conceptual. The selectors look for projects that demonstrate well thought out ideas, dealing sometimes with current issues, and innovative visual solutions that avoid clichés. The work that often cuts through is that which has distinctive visual appeal and poses intriguing questions as much as conveying resolved answers.

Categories

Much contemporary creative photography subtly challenges and utilises traditional genre distinctions such as fine art, science, still-life, fashion, advertising, landscape, portraiture, documentary, the record picture, the snapshot, etc. Apparently 'straight' documentary images may in fact be elaborately staged; what might at first glance appear as a fashion shoot is revealed as a documentary project; and works of fine-art resemble scientific imaging.

The works in this book seemed to fall naturally into four broad sections that could absorb some traditional categories and accommodate a number of readings: Objects, Environment, Identity and Photojournalism. Of course, there is some overlap between these categories, and certain works could occupy more than one. Yet, they provide us with a useful structure and there are common threads connecting the projects in these non-chronological groupings. The shared themes and concerns are a reflection of some of the most current pre-occupations in contemporary photographic practice.

Objects

The seemingly straight depiction of humble objects before the lens in the tradition of a still life has always been fertile territory for photographers. Lighting and staging play tricks with scale, and even the smallest item can appear like a monumental work of sculpture. There is something perhaps about the precision of making considered object ensembles that leads to a refinement in the consideration of tonality and printing of the works grouped in this section.

Isolating objects magnifies an uncanny feeling of their significance and physical presence, as in the work of Veronica Bailey, Kevin Newark and Indre Serpytyte. In each of these photographers' works, the factual rendition of the commonplace paradoxically provokes intrigue and mystery, secrets kept or revealed. Similarly, not all is what it seems in Emma Hamilton's apparently conventional still-life images: look again for a shocking surprise. A quest for equilibrium is found in the photographs of Sarah Lynch, where a stage is set for Lilliputian dramas, at once comic and existential. Elaborate staging and ensembles of objects are explored from different angles in the controlled palettes of Nicky Walsh and Danny Treacy. While Walsh suggests an austere corporate universality, Treacy's *Grey Area*, offers a neutral space for personal projection, a linguistic and visual metaphor that also challenges the convention of 'black and white' photography.

Identity

Photography has proved to be especially adept at examining notions of identity. The gap between the idea of how a person intends to present themselves and how they actually appear to the viewer is the creative tension underlying the classic photographs of August Sander and Diane Arbus. Alongside these historical precursors, more recent examples such as the work of Cindy Sherman, Nan Goldin and Rineke Dijkstra have acted as a touchstone for emergent practitioners seeking to probe the myriad meanings and messages created the moment a person poses for the camera.

Linking the work of Jerwood Award winners Travis Hodges, Moira Lovell, James Pogson and Luke Stephenson is the questioning of boundaries between personal and group identity: in their photographs, individuals dress distinctively to indicate their inclusion in a particular group. The sitter's attire is worn as a means of empowerment, a disguise or mask. Even a slight facial expression, or awkward bodily pose at odds with the disguise, causes slippage between the intended visual signal and its result. Such photographs can often reveal the chink in the armour of assumed bravado or sexual display, allegiance to a style or subculture. Various twists towards this approach in examining identity is provided by Oliver Parker, whose *Foxhounds* provides an uncannily anthropomorphic look at canine portraiture, and by Peter Oetzmann, who deconstructs and reveals the conventions of the photographic studio setting. Ed Kevill-Davies' series *Puppet Love* plays wittily with the conventions of family portraits, simultaneously documenting the dying art of ventriloquism. And since we cannot see their faces clearly, Alice Myers' images of children launching themselves into a swimming pool, as if embarking on a future metaphorical journey into life, are portraits intuited through posture, to be read as if they were lines in the palm. Tracing the life-journey, and the context of the environment in which it is lived, is the subject of Nina Mangalanayagam's tender portrait of her father. Here, the person and location seem to merge, leading us away from the concentration on the figure towards the environment as an indicator of emotional and spiritual resonance.

Environment

In the hands of a perceptive and sensitive artist, the landscape or urban environment is as much a psychological as a physical place. Locations we may normally ignore or pass by are transformed through the act of photographing them. This can be done through the practical and stylistic choices of photographic format, technique, exposure, angle and printing, coupled with the all-important mediating mindset of the eye and intellect behind the lens.

Edgar Martins finds the uncanny in the everyday in his evocatively-titled *Black Holes & Other Inconsistencies*, while Richard Page, Zoe Hatziyannaki and Paul Winch-Furness deal in various ways with similar issues of urban and suburban dislocation, town planning gone awry and the culture of surveillance. These themes also permeate Sarah Pickering's *Public Order* series, unsettling visual puzzles that depict what looks like a film stage set, which it is not, even if a dramatic performance of sorts is enacted in this location. All of these photographers' envisaged hybrid and marginal places use the visual language of fragmentation to weave their magic.

More ancient, natural landscapes are the subjects of other artists here, such as Daniel Gustav Cramer, whose *Woodland* images are redolent of mythical rather than real places. Martina Lindqvist's *Rågskär Island* takes the notion of a fantasy environment to its natural conclusion – these mysterious twilight scenes evoke and enhance the memory and essence of terrain through the clever use of family snapshots and miniature models. These photographs convey a sense of isolation and infer spatial and temporal displacement. Such philosophical issues underlie the works of Naglaa Walker, where images are to be read like the formula of a physics equation. In their own unique ways, each of these photographers conjures an environment that is part way between reality and fantasy, prose and poetry, the natural and the invented.

Photojournalism

Some of the most powerful and emotive photography mixes a refined visual sensibility with the gift of economical and urgent story-telling. Arguably, the golden age of photojournalism was from the 1930s to the 1950s, a period coinciding with global political and social upheaval and war that provided the staple subjects for photographers. During this time, the formation of Magnum Photos agency and the rise of the illustrated topical magazines such as *Paris Match*, *Picture Post* and *Life* provided an outlet for the work being produced. Gritty reportage developed and continued into the 1960s and '70s with features in the newspaper supplements, such as the *Sunday Times* magazine.

In the television age, and now in the internet and digital era, there is perhaps less scope for the traditional channels of agencies and picture magazines for photojournalism to make its voice heard. One result is that the language of photojournalism has crossed boundaries into other genres of photography – such as fine art practice, documentary and street photography – blurring and yet creatively mixing the dialogue. The photographers grouped here under the heading of 'photojournalism' have differing approaches and visual styles and may not strictly adhere to the pure sense of the genre. What binds them is a sense of being alert and intuitive, tuned in and responding to current issues: Sophie Gerrard reports on the pressing topic of environmentalism by focusing on the global traffic in electronic waste that ends up polluting India; Polly Braden examines manufacture in China by looking at the individuals that make up its vast workforce, while Kurt Tong records the country's 'People's Parks' that have recently fallen into a melancholic state of disrepair as young people seek entertainment elsewhere. Leisure and social time and its locations is also one of the main subjects of Léonie Purchas's photographs; but layers of complexity are added by the wider geographical setting of Israeli territory under conflict. As at the beginnings of photojournalism, troubled locations and situations provide motivation for those with a keen social conscience. Dana Popa's series of images dealing with the disturbing subject of sex trafficking in Moldova is sensitively and emotively done. Personal stories are used to tell the bigger narrative of shattered families and exploitation based in one country but leaving a trail across Europe. Photojournalism, and its related photographic forms, continues to probe the topical issues of our times, posing political as well as moral questions, and challenging us to take a personal standpoint.

Influences

The best practitioners have understood their position in the history of the medium with increasing sophistication. The knowing use of quotation, irony, parody and self-reference is evident in some of the work discussed and reproduced here. Others have trodden a careful path through their visual and theoretical influences, assimilating and modifying them to create something that speaks to the viewer with an individual voice. Their works have become aligned with the overriding conceptual practices of fine art; but they have not lost sight of technique and craft. On one hand, increasingly prevalent digital technology has allowed innovative methods of production and dissemination. On the other, perhaps as a reaction to the advent of digital, traditional chemistry-based techniques have been newly appraised. This has led to a subtle appreciation and deployment of the various modes of photographic style and genre available to the modern practitioner, matching and enhancing the conceptual message alongside the hallmarks of personal identity.

Contexts

The recent popularity of photography and its dominance within contemporary art can be understood by looking at several interrelated philosophical and very practical changes, including: technique and presentation, collecting and the art market, publishing and critical writing in books and magazines, endorsement and visibility in galleries and museums and teaching in colleges. Since the late 1980s, overwhelmingly, the increase in the sheer size of photographic exhibition prints has become a notable factor. They are able to 'hold the wall' and compete with the impact and scale of other works of contemporary art in large, white gallery spaces. The size also allows the viewer to become engrossed in the image and its details. Colour printing has become the dominant choice; this is reflected in the work of the Jerwood Photography Award winners. Throughout the last ten years, private collectors, galleries and art fairs created and sustained a market. Fears that photography is a medium of mass reproduction, and is therefore devalued by its multiplicity, have been assuaged through the market's regulatory device of limited edition and fine prints. A new kind of private collector is perhaps less daunted by photography than more traditional art forms and is drawn by the modernity, accessibility and familiarity of photographic images – as well as the deep underlying subtlety that can be derived from the best works. Even taking recent global economic troubles into account, there is no doubt that the appetite for photographs and their relative market value, compared to twenty years ago, has increased a great deal. The market developed an awareness of the position of photography and its unique power outside the standard circles of fine art appreciation.

Photography has always looked good on the printed page. In fact the wider dissemination of photographic art has often been in the first instance through books rather than prints made for exhibition. Photography also works particularly well when seen in series, and books best facilitate this kind of viewing. Publishers and writers have produced informative and visually seductive books and journals in recent years that reinforce collecting and scholarship. Meanwhile, galleries and museums continue to stage larger and more frequent exhibitions featuring contemporary photography and to build archives of photographs. At the same time graduates from degree courses are schooled in the history, critical theory and technique of the medium. The Jerwood Award winners are themselves evidence of the best of individual talent coupled with excellent mentoring behind the scenes. Throughout these activities an increased consciousness of the exciting and complex aesthetic, historical and cultural positions of the photographic image has emerged and taken hold.

Future

The Jerwood Photography Awards offers support and a raised profile in the early stages of the careers of promising photographers' making their way into professional life. Some of them will go on to become major international artists in the field. It is heartening to have witnessed already the wider success of those winners of the earlier years of the Award who have had time to mature and explore their vision further and more deeply. I look forward each year to the discoveries of the Award with genuine excitement.

Photography commands great pathos with its ability to freeze time and place. Ultimately, it makes us aware of our inability to witness everything we might wish to during our own comparatively fleeting lives. Yet it has always had an enigmatic relationship with the 'real' world that it seems to depict. One of its most compelling aspects is its creative capacity to tangle fact with fiction. A photograph is always a translation of reality seen from the physical and conceptual standpoint of the person creating the image – as well as that of the viewer. It is for this reason that we need to seek and support the innovative image-makers of the future who translate and comment creatively on the world, enriching our visual and intellectual lives.

Martin Barnes is Senior Curator, Photographs, Victoria and Albert Museum, London.

Jerwood Photography Awards 2003 exhibition at Stills Gallery, Edinburgh International Festival, August 2004.

Works

Sarah Lynch
Suspended Realities, 2003

Suspended Realities is a series of table-top scenes meticulously constructed from the modest forms of small fruits and leaves. Using wire and paper as splints and supports, Sarah Lynch creates sculptural balancing acts that are overshadowed by the possibility of collapse or sudden motion. Emptying the landscape around these theatrical scenes allows them to take on an abstract and epic scale.

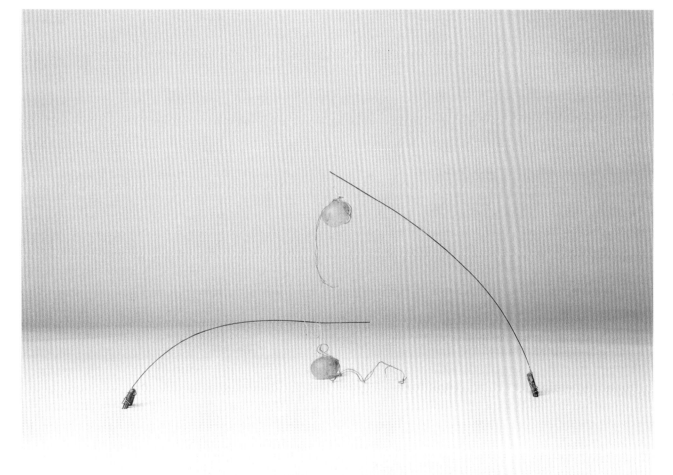

Veronica Bailey
2 Willow Road, 2003

'From Your Friends in Norway'
J W Eides Forlag
Bergen, Norway 1946

Veronica Bailey's series of magnified book edges were made within the library at the National Trust house, 2 Willow Road, London, the 1939 modernist house of architect Ernö Goldfinger. Reflecting a wealth of 20th century art, history and culture, the images form an alternative portrait of the private, but now public, lives of Goldfinger and his wife, artist Ursula Blackwell.

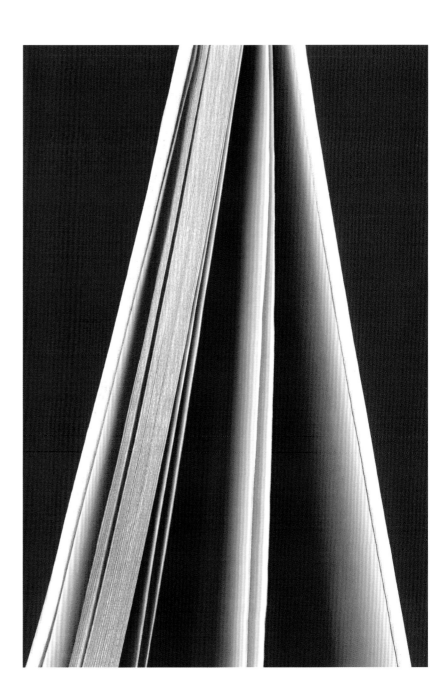

'A Look At My Life'
Eileen Agar
Methuen, London 1988

21

22

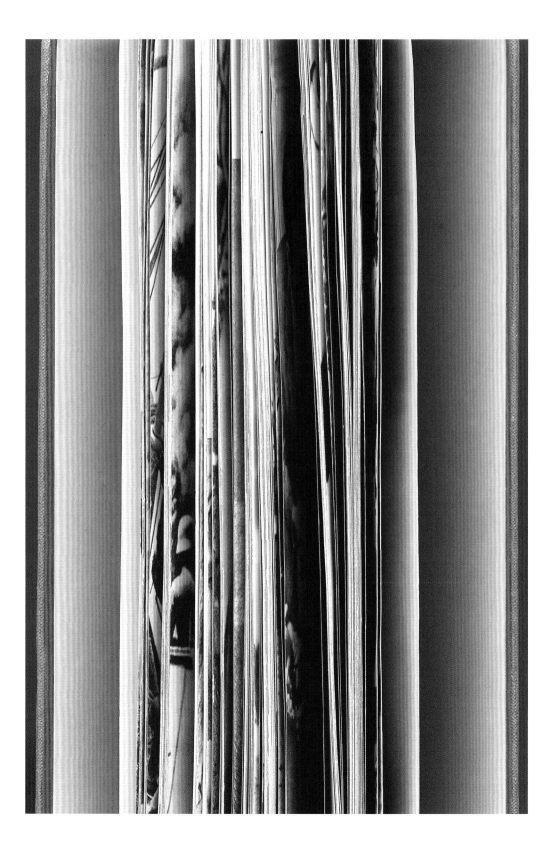

Danny Treacy
Grey Area, 2003

Danny Treacy's images are both literal and metaphorical 'grey areas'. By painstakingly painting these otherwise ordinary places, they become both beautified and fetishised. A symbolic colour in many cultures, grey is 'the colour of no colour', representing an ambiguous middle ground where possibilities are boundless.

Indre Serpytyte

A State of Silence, 2006

In *A State of Silence* Indre Serpytyte questions official accounts of the death of her father, a government official, in an apparent car accident. These striking still-life photographs – a typewriter, a telephone, a military hat – present the viewer with a narrative of intrigue. The document is shredded and the telephone silent, leaving what appears to be the remnants of a bureaucratic system.

Emma Hamilton
Flores Carneus, 2004

Emma Hamilton's *Flores Carneus* series presents bouquets of delicate flowers carefully sculpted from the flesh and organs of animals. The recognisable still-life composition draws the viewer in to reveal strange unknown landscapes of colour and texture. Provoking both visual pleasure and revulsion, these images present the materials of the body as objects for contemplation and morbid fascination.

Kevin Newark

Protoplasm, 2006

In *Protoplasm* Kevin Newark finds transcendent possibilities in plastic bags cast adrift in the canals of East London. His photographs indicate pressing current issues about waste and its knock-on global effects. These photographs transform the material momentarily into something precious, jewel-like, reminiscent of cells under a microscope or clouds of gas and matter in distant galaxies.

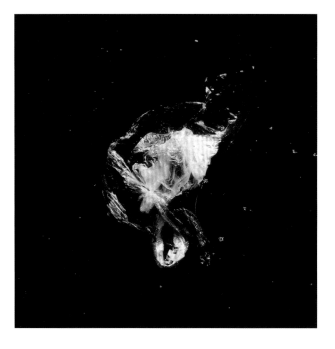

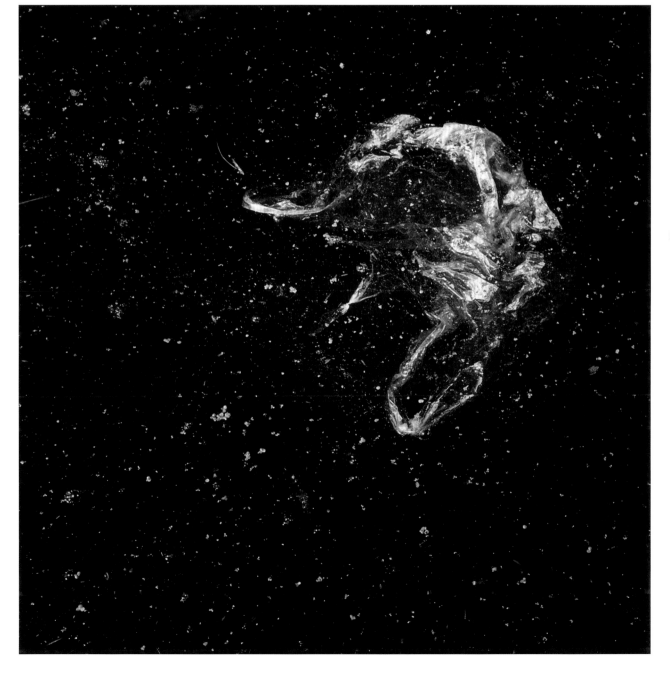

Nicky Walsh
Untitled, 2005–07

For Nicky Walsh, a limited palette and narrow tonal range are part of a deliberate, disciplined attempt to depict the most subtle differences in opacity and tonality of everyday objects. In this cool space of an anonymous office, expanses of pale greys and greens are broken occasionally by the hard black edge of a table or the metallic gleam of binder clips.

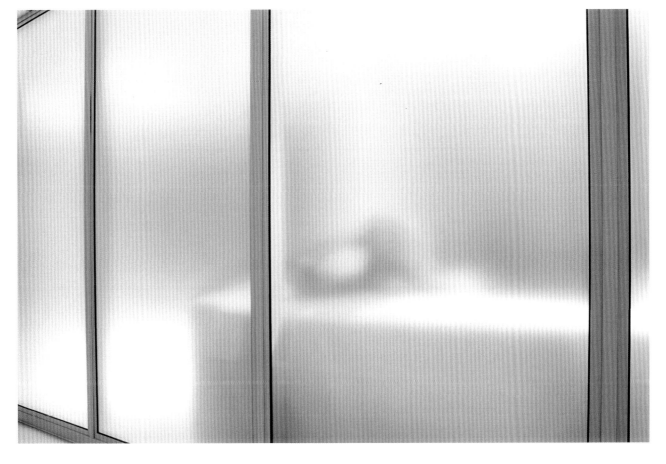

42

Peter Oetzmann
Picture This, 2005–06

In *Picture This,* Peter Oetzmann has recreated the romantic notion of the English landscape. Three large painted backdrops were taken into the street, and members of the public invited to step into the paintings to have their photographs taken. The final photographs make reference to a number of sources, from use of perspective in Renaissance art to the painted backdrops used by early photographers.

Nina Mangalanayagam

Snötäckt – the weight of the snow covered all of him, 2005

This series of portraits and landscapes narrates the life of Nina Mangalanayagam's father, a Sri Lankan émigré who lives in Sweden. Set against a backdrop of bleached, uncompromising landscapes, the artist's father is overtaken with ill health and will never see his homeland again. Mangalanayagam's photographs challenge the stereotype of the émigré, employing her personal narrative to explore wider issues of Diaspora.

Luke Stephenson
Spectacle wearing folk, 2005

Luke Stephenson's portrait series counteracts the received notion of portraiture – the search for visual truth. Redolent of portrait styles from instruction manuals and product catalogues, he has created comedic retro fantasies through a visual rhetoric of 1960s and '70s styling. Assuming personae dictated by the spectacles they wear, this beguiling cast of characters pose with mock gravity.

52

54

Moira Lovell

The After School Club, 2006–07

Moira Lovell's series shows young women taken from school-themed nightclubs and transported, still wearing their revellers' outfits, to the gates of their former schools. Through the adoption of an alternative persona, this nightclub phenomenon seems liberating, and yet is highly socially controlled. Dislocated from the night-time context of fancy dress, the women appear unsure of the role they must now play.

56

Travis Hodges

Dead Time, 2004

Travis Hodges' series *Dead Time* developed from accidental meetings with teenage boys on the streets of Falmouth. 'Dead time' refers to the time between dusk and sleep when these youths have nothing else to do other than loiter around. Separated out from their groups of friends, the boys let their aggressive poses partially relax, and allow other aspects of themselves to become visible.

Alice Myers
Rocket, 2008

Alice Myers' images record the very moment when a child pushes away from the side of a swimming pool, letting go of safety and launching into the unknown; a simultaneously frightening and exhilarating experience. The event is shared with the viewer who, in the position of adult or parent, watches from above as their child lets go of safety.

James Pogson

Ladykillers, 2007

The series *Ladykillers* takes its title from the event at which these portraits were made, an international women's Thai kickboxing tournament held in England in 2008. Formerly banned in Thailand, women's kickboxing remains a subcategory of a sport dominated by male competitors. Photographed either before or immediately after they compete, the women appear preoccupied and, even when their gaze is directed at the camera, they do not seem to engage with the photographer or – by extension – the viewer.

Ed Kevill-Davies

Puppet Love, 2006–07

The series *Puppet Love* explores the special relationship a ventriloquist shares with his puppet. These portraits feature some of the last remaining practising ventriloquists in the UK, and aim to show how the dedication of so much of the ventriloquist's time to his puppet affects his home life and his relationship with his other family members.

74

Oliver Parker

Foxhounds, 2005

In this series Oliver Parker has photographed foxhounds posed in studio-shoot conditions, removed from their natural environment. Employing the visual rhetoric of the portrait, the hounds are removed from the political and social debate that raises uncertainty about the future of the breed and ultimately the tradition of fox hunting.

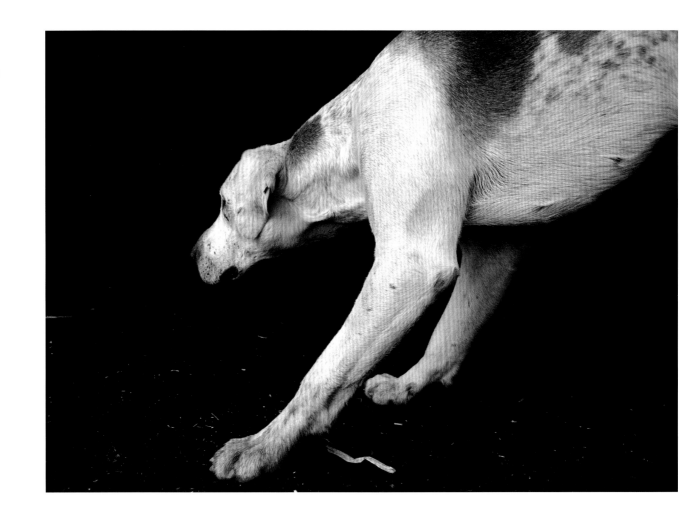

Zoe Hatziyannaki

Regeneration Stories, 2006

Produced at two of the most familiar regenerated areas of London, Zoe Hatziyannaki's *Regeneration Stories* captures the idealisation of urban space, demonstrating the perfect outcome of planning. This controlled and orderly view is questioned, however, by the enlarged portraits of passers-by, the blurred effect evocative of CCTV cameras that are common to urban areas such as these.

Sarah Pickering

Public Order, 2002–05

Sarah Pickering's *Public Order* series documents the ambiguous landscape of the Metropolitan Police Public Order Training Centre, a constructed world of civic intransigence and imagined threat. Pickering's conceptual photo-reportage explores this strange reconstructed world of dereliction: the nightclub has no windows or doors and behind a row of terraced houses there is only air and space.

84

Naglaa Walker

On Physics, 2001

Naglaa Walker's diptychs contrast images of scientific equations chalked onto a blackboard with staged photographs of people engaging in everyday situations. Instead of providing an illustrated diagram alongside the equations, Walker's photographs present people enacting the role of objects, planets and electrons.

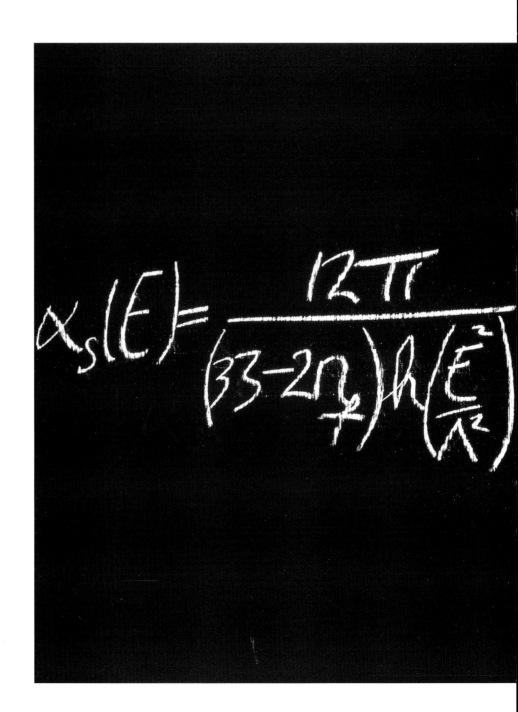

Strong Interaction (Quantum Chromodynamics): The strong coupling parameter between two quarks depends on the flavours present
– the particles must maintain some distance between them in order to retain their strong attraction.

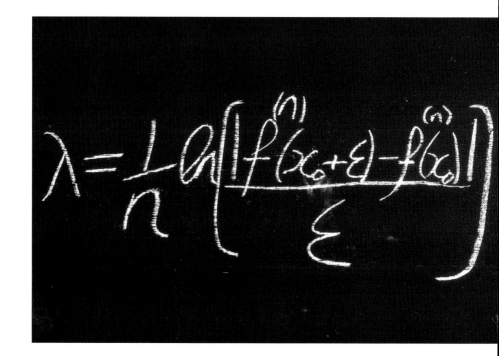

$$\lambda = \frac{1}{n} \ln \left[\frac{|f^{(n)}(x_0 + \varepsilon) - f^{(n)}(x_0)|}{\varepsilon} \right]$$

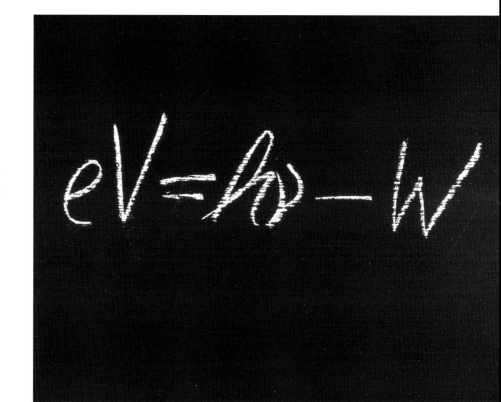

$$eV = \hbar\omega - W$$

Edgar Martins

Black Holes & Other Inconsistencies, 2002

In the series *Black Holes & Other Inconsistencies* Edgar Martins takes the viewer on a journey through a dream-like landscape. The urban spaces in his photographs are presented as fragile, transient and fragmented. Like black holes, these places suggest that boundaries are temporary and space is permeable.

Richard Page
Suburban Exposures, 2003

In *Suburban Exposures,* Richard Page explores psychological spaces on the edges of ordinary residential areas. Through compositional manipulation of the landscape, these images are imbued with an uncanny quality in which familiar territory becomes unfamiliar. The standardised neighbourhoods are distorted, viewed from the edges as if by a stranger.

96

Martina Lindqvist
Rågskär Island, 2008

The series *Rågskär Island* depicts the small island off the coast of Finland that Martina Lindqvist visited as a child each summer. Seemingly made at twilight, these images are not in fact direct recordings of an actual place, but photographs of miniature models that Lindqvist constructs after family snapshots, in which enlarged prints of the original snapshots form the backdrop.

Paul Winch-Furness
The Master Plan, 2006

Paul Winch-Furness has photographed Milton Keynes, the ultimate planned environment, using camera movements to distort the perspective of the scene. The photographs, devoid of people, as in the original architects' model, ask the viewer to assess the design and construction of the town, reversing the usual process of model to conception, and to consider whether the vision of the town planners, as set out in the 1970 Master Plan, is achieved.

Daniel Gustav Cramer

Woodland, 2005

An ongoing project over a number of years, Daniel Gustav Cramer's series *Woodland* documents forestland across continents, uncovering a secret, hidden and obscure world. Journeying like an explorer into the dense canopy of forestland from Big Sur in California to the Black Forest in Germany, he searches out the dark centre.

Polly Braden
Made in China, 2003

Polly Braden's colour photographs are from a series documenting a factory in Selena, Quangdong, China, that produces shoes for sale in high street shops. The photographs tell the story of the pressurised working and living conditions of Ho Ping and her co-workers and the reality behind anonymous Western chain store labels.

Working in the shoe factory,
Selena, 2003 *(right)*

New recruits sing
team-building songs in their
training week, 2003 *(below)*

Dormitories at the factory where all the workers sleep, 2003 *(left)*
Queuing for the factory bus on their day off, 2003 *(below)*

Kurt Tong
People's Park, 2007

The *People's Park* series was inspired by the artist's family snapshots and childhood memories of Hong Kong. He has photographed city parks in mainland China similar to those of his youth, recording areas that were once main focal points of cities in the Communist era, where families had their outings and couples met. Today, however, as the Chinese economy expands, many families seek entertainment elsewhere, and the parks have fallen into disrepair.

Dana Popa

Not Natasha, 2006

Not Natasha traces the tragically fractured and damaged lives of young girls and women caught up in human trafficking for prostitution within Europe. Dana Popa is a native of Romania, and her focus is on women who originate from the neighbouring Republic of Moldova, the poorest nation in Europe and the main source of sex slaves for the whole continent. Each year, at least 500 women return to Moldova, broken and traumatised from the experience.

Elena, 23 years old, August 2006.
"I thought I would work purely as a vendor at the market in Moscow for $200 a month… Instead I got sold and resold to pimps until a client set me free…"

Maria only wanted to save money for her wedding. Her fiancé abandoned her on the grounds that the baby she gave birth to after she escaped from the traffickers was not his child

Dalia, 20 years old, August 2006.
Moments before a gynaecological examination, at the International Organisation of Migration in Moldova. Dalia was trafficked to Turkey and forced into prostitution for three months.

123

Sophie Gerrard

E-wasteland – The growing problem of e-waste in India, 2006

Photographed in workshops and recycling yards on the outskirts of Mumbai, Chennai, Bangalore and Delhi, Sophie Gerrard's images starkly reveal the local and human impact of the West's race for ever-newer information technology and, by implication, the global ramifications of consumer culture.

A boy looks out over a pool of polluted water to a pile of discarded circuit boards, Mandoli, India, 2006 *(left)*
E-waste 'cooking' in acid to collect heavy metals, Seelampur, India, 2006 *(below)*

Léonie Purchas
Escape in Israel, 2004

Inspired by the rise of tourism in Israel, Léonie Purchas set out to explore the behaviour of these visitors by documenting their activities. *Escape in Israel* presents a series of cathartic rituals, both public and private, that are carried out by ordinary people against the background of life in Israel. The photographs were made at various locations, including Eilat, a tourist resort that has never experienced conflict.

Jerwood Photography Awards 2007 exhibition at the Jerwood Space, London.
Seminar on 19 November 2007, chaired by Martin Barnes, with Kevin Newark, Sophie Gerrard, Moira Lovell and Ed Kevill-Davies. (Photo: Sarah Williams)

Afterword
Gloria Chalmers

In 2002 when Roanne Dods invited Portfolio Magazine to devise a photography awards scheme for the Jerwood Charitable Foundation, we recommended five equal Awards to artist photographers during the first few years following graduation, to be selected by a changing group of curators, writers, publishers and visual artists. Five equal awards for originality and excellence, and no overall winner, would ensure an emphasis on a range of photographic practices, and equal recognition for graduates of both BA and MA degree courses.

In each of the six years of the Awards, we viewed at least 500 portfolios of up to ten photographs each. The first year's winners in 2003 were all graduates of MA courses in London, but in each of the subsequent years it transpired that original and mature work was being submitted by young graduates from BA courses throughout the UK. As each year introduced the work of so many talented applicants, we at Portfolio recognised the high standards and rigour of photography degree courses in the UK, and the magazine was delighted to publish so much outstanding new work identified through the Award selection process.

The Awards have created a platform for innovative photography that challenged conventions, with some of the most creative portfolios being inspired by the personal histories of the artists. Socially engaged work was also perceived to be strong each year, with many of the winners producing fresh, new perspectives on contemporary issues.

Each year the work of the winners was presented at an awards evening at the Jerwood Space in London, with the exhibition then touring to other UK galleries. These exhibitions were accompanied by talks, seminars and portfolio viewing sessions, offering the winners the opportunity to engage with audiences and to gain experience in public speaking. Each year the five would appear to forge a close group identity and support each other on practical and emotional levels, often the more experienced mentoring the younger winners, with lasting friendships created in the process. When winners discuss the impact of winning a Jerwood Photography Award they consistently cite the opportunity to invest in equipment, the gaining of personal confidence, selection for group and solo exhibitions, gallery representation and the sale of prints to collectors, with many of the winners also achieving international success.

I would like to take this opportunity to thank the Jerwood Charitable Foundation for their generous support of the photography awards, their recognition of the importance of photography within contemporary visual arts and the impact that these awards have made on the developing careers of emerging artists. We are also fortunate to have had the opportunity to work with such dedicated selectors over the years, who have given so generously of their time and expertise. And I am especially grateful to Roanne Dods and Thomas Ponsonby for their extensive knowledge, their constant enthusiasm for the Awards' processes and outcomes, and their personal commitment to supporting a new generation of artist photographers.

Finally, I would like to say that the Jerwood Photography Awards are an exciting, illuminating and, above all, rewarding method of supporting new photographic art, and I am delighted that we at Portfolio are able to present the work of the winners in this thematic format, as *New Light*.

Gloria Chalmers is Editor of Portfolio Magazine.

List of Works

Veronica Bailey
Born in London, England, 1965.
Lives and works in London.
MA Communication Design, Central Saint Martins College, London, 2003

2 Willow Road, 2003
Durst lambda prints, 59.4 x 42 cm, 84.1 x 59.4 cm
and 118.9 x 84.1 cm

Polly Braden
Born in Perth, Scotland, 1974.
Lives and works in London.
PG (Dip) Photojournalism, London College of Communication, London, 2002

Made in China, 2003
C-type prints, 12 x 16 inches

Daniel Gustav Cramer
Born in Neuss, Germany, 1975
Lives and works in London and Berlin.
MA Photography, Royal College of Art, London, 2003

Woodland, 2005
C-type prints, 105 x 105 cm, Edition of 5

Sophie Gerrard
Born in Edinburgh, Scotland, 1978. Lives and works in London.
MA Photojournalism and Documentary Photography, London College of Communication, London, 2006

E-wasteland, 2006
C-type prints, 50 x 50 cm, Edition of 10
Courtesy The Photographers' Gallery, London

Emma Hamilton
Born in Stirling, Scotland, 1981. Lives and works in Stirling.
BA (Hons) Drawing and Painting, Duncan of Jordanstone College of Art and Design, Dundee, 2004

Flores Carneus, 2004
Cibachrome prints, 30 x 40 inches

Zoe Hatziyannaki
Born in Athens, Greece, 1976.
PhD Visual Cultures, Goldsmiths College, London (2006-10)
MA Photography and Urban Cultures, Goldsmiths College, London, 2005

Regeneration Stories, 2006
C-type prints, 32.5 x 80 cm, Edition of 10

Travis Hodges
Born in Cape Town, South Africa, 1981.
Lives and works in London.
BA (Hons) Falmouth College of Arts, Cornwall, 2004

Dead Time, 2004
C-type prints, 14 x 14 inches

Ed Kevill-Davies
Born in England, 1984.
Lives and works in London.
BA (Hons) Photography, London College of Communication, London, 2007

Puppet Love, 2006–07
C-type prints, 75 x 75 cm

Martina Lindqvist
Born in Umeå, Sweden, 1981.
Lives and works in London.
BA (Hons) Photographic Arts, University of Westminster, London, 2008

Rågskär Island, 2008
Lambda prints, 61.25 x 76.25 cm, Edition of 7

Moira Lovell
Born in Doncaster, England 1977.
Lives and works in London.
Associate Lecturer at Southampton Solent University
MA Photography, London College of Communication, London, 2006

The After School Club, 2006–07
C-type digital prints, 50.5 x 72.5 cm

Sarah Lynch
Born in London, England, 1977.
Lives and works in Barcelona, Spain.
MA Photography, Edinburgh College of Art, Edinburgh, 2003

Suspended Realities, 2003
Giclée digital prints on cotton finish paper,
44 x 36 and 27 x 33 inches

Nina Mangalanayagam
Born in Lund, Sweden, 1980.
Lives and works in London.
MA Photography, Royal College of Art, London, 2007-09
BA (Hons) Photography, London College of Communication, London, 2005

Snötäckt (the weight of the snow covered all of him), 2005
C-type Prints, 100 x 100 cm and 50 x 50 cm

Edgar Martins
Born Évora, Portugal, 1977.
Lives and works in England.
MA Photography, Royal College of Art, London, 2002

Black Holes and Other Inconsistencies, 2002
C-type prints, 66 x 83 cm

Alice Myers
Born in Lancaster, England, 1986.
Lives and works in Edinburgh.
BA (Hons) Photography, Edinburgh College of Art, Edinburgh, 2008

Rocket, 2008
Digital C-type prints, 60 x 60 cm, Edition of 12

Kevin Newark
Born in Saskatoon, Saskatchewan, Canada, 1973.
Lives and works in London. He teaches at MPW London.
MA Photography, London College of Communication, London, 2006

Protoplasm, 2006
C-type prints, 35 x 35 cm

Peter Oetzmann
Born in Kent, England, 1978.
Currently lives and works in Mongolia.
MA Photography, University College for the Creative Arts,
Rochester, 2006
Picture This, 2005-06
Digital Inkjet prints, 100 x 96 cm

Richard Page
Born in Bournemouth, England, 1975.
Lives and works in Cardiff. Senior Lecturer in Photography
at Swansea Metropolitan University.
MA Photographic Studies, University of Westminster,
London, 2003
Suburban Exposures, 2003-04
Fujitrans prints in lightboxes, Series of 8

Oliver Parker
Born in Banbury, England, 1980.
Lives and works in London.
BA (Hons) Photography, Nottingham Trent University,
Nottingham, 2005
Foxhounds, 2005
Lambda digital prints, 70 x 50 cm

Sarah Pickering
Born in Durham, England, 1972.
Lives and works in London.
Teaching Fellow at the Slade School of Art, London.
MA Photography, Royal College of Art, London, 2005
Public Order, 2002–05
C-type prints, 76cm x 94cm, Edition of 5,
Courtesy Meessen De Clercq, Brussels

James Pogson
Born in Scunthorpe, England, 1984.
Lives and works in London.
BA (Hons) Photography, University of Staffordshire,
Stoke-on-Trent, 2008
Ladykillers, 2008
Digital C-type prints, 60 x 50 cm, Edition of 10

Dana Popa
Born in Bacau, Romania, 1977.
Lives and works in London.
MA Photojournalism and Documentary Photography,
London College of Communication, London, 2006
Not Natasha, 2006
C-type prints, 20 x 24 inches

Léonie Purchas
Born in London, 1978.
Lives and works in London.
PG (Dip) Photojournalism, London College of Communication,
London, 2003
Escape in Israel, 2004
C-type prints, 16 x 20 inches

Indre Serpytyte
Born in Palanga, Lithuania, 1983.
Lives and works in London.
MA Photography, Royal College of Art, London, 2007-09
BA Editorial Photography, University of Brighton,
Brighton, 2006
A State of Silence, 2006
C-type prints, 50 x 60 cm

Luke Stephenson
Born in Darlington, England, 1983.
Lives and works in London.
BA (Hons) Photography, Blackpool and the Flyde College,
Blackpool, 2005
Spectacle wearing folk, 2005
C-type prints, 14 x 14 inches

Kurt Tong
Born in Hong Kong, 1977.
Lives and works in London.
MA Photojournalism and Documentary Photography,
London College of Communication, London, 2007
People's Park, 2007
Lambda prints, 60 x 75 cm, Edition of 10
80 x 100 cm, Edition of 5

Danny Treacy
Born in Manchester, England, 1975.
Lives and works in London.
Associate Lecturer, Camberwell College of Arts, London.
MA Photography, Royal College of Art, London, 2002
Grey Area, 2003
Archival Lambda prints, 150 x 120 cm

Naglaa Walker
Born in Cairo, Egypt, 1970. Lives and works in London.
MA Photography, Royal College of Art, London, 2003
On Physics, 2001
R-type diptych, 20 x 24 inches each
combined size 42 x 24 inches

Nicky Walsh
Born in Cardiff, Wales, 1979.
Lives and works in London.
MA Photography, University of Brighton, 2007
Untitled, 2005-07
Digital C-type prints, 75 x 75 cm and 75 x 100 cm,
Edition of 10

Paul Winch-Furness
Born in London, England, 1970.
Lives and works in London.
Lecturer in Photography, Westminster University, London.
BA (Hons) Photography, University of Westminster,
London, 2006
The Master Plan, 2006
C-type digital prints, 84 x 70 cm

New Light
Jerwood Photography Awards 2003-08

Published in April 2009
by Portfolio Magazine
43 Candlemaker Row
Edinburgh EH1 2QB
Scotland

Tel: (00) 44 131 220 1911
Email: mag@portfoliocatalogue.com
www.portfoliocatalogue.com

Editor:
Gloria Chalmers

Designer:
Patricia Bartie

Cover photograph:
Sarah Lynch, Suspended Realities (Untitled No. 1) 2003

Reprographics and Printing:
Provided and Sponsored by Team Impression, Leeds

Paper: Consort Royal Silk 150 gsm
Howard Smith Paper (Scotland) Limited

Distribution: Central Books
99 Wallis Road, London E9 5LN
(44) 0845 458 9911
www.centralbooks.com

Portfolio Magazine is financially supported by Scottish Arts Council.

Acknowledgements:
Portfolio Magazine acknowledges the contribution of the artists and selectors, and gives special thanks to the following individuals and organisations for their valuable support during the Jerwood Photography Awards 2003-08: Roanne Dods, Thomas Ponsonby, Sarah Williams, Patricia Bartie, Mary Ann Kennedy, David Alan Mellor, Andrew Wolffe, Tom Kennedy, Elizabeth Pardoe, Victoria Viola, Parker Harris, Team Impression, Genesis Imaging and Spectrum Photographic.

ISBN 978-0-9520608-4-0